MAKE

THEM

GROW

by

Giving Feedback People Apply

Michal Nowostawski

Make Them Grow
by Giving Feedback People Apply

Copyright © 2016 by Michal Nowostawski

All Rights Reserved

No part of this publication may be reproduced, distributed, or transmitted in any form or by any means, including photocopying, recording, or other electronic or mechanical methods without the prior written permission of the publisher, except in the case of brief quotations embodied in critical reviews and certain other noncommercial uses permitted by copyright law.

Disclaimer

All the material contained in this book is provided for educational and informational purposes only. No responsibility can be taken for any results or outcomes resulting from the use of this material.

While every attempt has been made to provide information that is both accurate and effective, the author does not assume any responsibility for the accuracy or use/misuse of this information.

Table of Contents

I. Introduction 4

II. Feedback Effectiveness 9

III. Forms of Feedback 13

IV. Why You Should Give Feedback To Others 16

V. Four Rules of Effective Feedback 19

VI. The Techniques for Constructing Feedback 31

VII. Providing Feedback on Positive Behaviors 40

VIII. Providing Feedback on Negative Behaviors 49

IX. Receiving Feedback 57

X. Summary 66

I. Introduction

A few years ago there was an experiment conducted based on the fact that the volunteers had to perform some work. Each of them received a card on which there were scattered random letters. Their task was to find a pair of identical letters. For the execution of the task, they received a small financial gratification. After finishing work, the researcher asked them a question, if they want ed to perform again the same work with a different card, for a little less money. The experiment lasted until respondent said he did not want to look for pairs anymore. The study was divided into three variants. In the first one, respondent wrote his name on a piece of paper, marked pairs and gave the card to the researcher. He looked at the card, said *aha*, and put it off on the side. In the second variant, the subject didn't write his name on a piece of paper and a researcher, without looking at it, right away postponed it aside. In the third variant, the researcher was putting it directly to a shredder without looking at it.

What were the effects of all three cases? In the first case, people worked the longest, which means they performed the work for much lower remuneration. In the case of the destruction of the results of their work as well as in the absence of interest in their work, the effect was very similar. People much faster discouraged to perform given action.

What this experiment teaches us in the context of feedback is that the lack of interest in the effort put by people, brings similar effects as the blatant destruction of their work. But short *aha* can rise the motivation to work significantly. Therefore, think of what can be achieved by providing employees with valuable feedback about what they are doing. Think also about how easy it is to discourage people at their jobs if you do not give them any information.

Both of above situations, I experienced firsthand while working as an Agile Coach at a medium-sized company. It was not an experiment, but something that took place in real conditions. At first, I had a boss who was interested in my work and provided me with feedback on how I work. Although there was a lot of praise, that there were also situations where I was reprimanded. In both cases, however, I knew that my work is useful and it is something to develop. I wanted to be better every day and in a couple of months, I've achieved outstanding results. But after an organizational structure has changed, my boss changed as well. The new manager had no idea about work I do, so he left me to my own devices. For several months I hadn't received any information about how I do my job. Feedback deprivation made me lost the sense of what I was doing. My growth really slowed down and it was much harder to find new challenges. Motivation was lower than ever.

I share this story with you, because I think feedback is really underrated in most companies which leads to demotivation of workers. But, I do not want you to just read about it. I want you to feel it on your own. Just remember the time, when you were a kid, how you felt playing and building a construction out of Lego bricks? Your parents looked at you and said *really nice work*. You wanted to impress them even more, so you started to build something better to get their appreciation again. This led you to superior results in bricks building. Or perhaps it was painting in your case, or cooking, or another activity at which you were immersed as a child. Every time somebody paid attention to what you did and gave you a feedback, you wanted to do it better. This mechanism works exactly the same in adult life when we carry out our activities. Quick feedback is essential for people to grow, excel, and in the end, to surprise others with outstanding results.

Think about the results you can achieve by giving people a simple feedback on their contribution to the development of the company. It is relatively easy to do, but if you want to do it even more effectively, read this book to the end. It's all about giving perfect feedback in any situation. The feedback that won't be rejected immediately, but will be applied or at least thought over.

I wrote this book based on my personal experience and that of others at work and in everyday life. As a team coach in a tech company, I have had to deal with feedback and its influence on the performance of teams and individuals. I know exactly how feedback and the culture of openness can affect the morale of a team and its performance. I also know the negative effects of poorly expressed feedback. I have seen cases of manipulation, where praises are showered just before a request to do something. I have also seen the confusion of people when the „sandwich" method was used (positive, negative, positive) on them. Afterward, such an individual will have no idea what he was doing well or otherwise. Finally, I have experienced firsthand both the lack of any feedback on my work and the effect of people's appreciation for my contributions.

It's my desire that companies are aware of the power of feedback so they begin to appreciate it. It not only contributes to an increase in employee satisfaction but also delivers financial benefits. It is worth mentioning that there are several factors that make organizations reluctant to apply a policy of openness. This may include the prevailing beliefs, the environment, the work culture, or a lack of skills. This book aims to tackle the last one: a lack of skills. It shows how to communicate feedback to others effectively.

This book is, therefore, for anyone interested in personal development and in the development of those around him. You can build better organizations through the implementation of feedback as a primary tool of communication and development. The culture of openness does not have to go from the top down. Of course, it should and if it goes like that, things become a lot easier. But I have seen teams which worked out their own culture in which passing information on mutual activities was the norm and this had a tremendous impact on their productivity and satisfaction.

On the other hand, all those who want to better communicate their needs to others every day will also benefit from this book. The rules included here will also be useful to parents in raising their children. With the tips included, they will be able to build relationships with their children more effectively and help them grow to become successful individuals.

II. Feedback Effectiveness

Have you ever wondered why online courses or advice in the form of handbooks are much less effective than courses taught in a classroom? Or why there is a big difference in the amount of time taken to learn the basics of a foreign language from a book as compared to learning in front of a teacher? The same knowledge is given in both settings. So, why this difference in the rate of learning?

The difference between these two methods of learning is the frequency and speed of receiving feedback, that is, information about your progress. When you practice at home or from a textbook, you lose many hours making mistakes repeatedly that could have easily been corrected if you had an immediate feedback. For example, if you are learning a foreign language from a textbook, you will likely pronounce a word incorrectly a number of times. Whereas, in a class, you will be corrected almost immediately. This will save you time and unnecessary frustrations from making unneeded mistakes. Such an instant feedback effectively gives you hours, weeks and even months of accelerating the development of specific skill. This concept of feedback is applicable to work as well. Sometimes employee repeats a behavior for months in a belief that she is doing the right thing. However, a second opinion from you surely open her eyes to some changes she might need to make. Think of how much time she lost because of doing a job the wrong way. The sooner you provide a feedback the more time will be spent on doing things correctly. And no matter what the feedback is, it will keep motivation high as you are interested in what she is doing. Being truly involved in what your employees has already done is half a success. Giving them a constructive feedback on their job will take them to the next level.

Imagine that you are at a party where you are conversing with a woman who has smeared makeup on her face. She probably made a careless gesture earlier at the party and a streak of black gunk was rubbed on her cheek. Would you tell her? You may choose not to tell her to avoid an awkward situation or feel silly. You will continue a nice conversation without a feedback. This woman will then go home after the party and discover that she had a smeared makeup all through the party. She will feel very bad and start to wonder from which moment she looked like that. All the good experiences from the party will be marred by this minor occurrence.

However, if, during your conversation, you told her about her smudged makeup, you will save her the pains of feeling bad about the makeup. You can be sure that she will go to the restroom and in a moment (or moments) later, appear with makeup as perfect as she had on from the very beginning of the event. And you will be her hero that changed her fate for the day.

This illustration is just to show what a feedback is. On the one hand, if it is given to you, you can use it to develop yourself in a particular skill. Treat it like a gift, something, to think of or to apply if needed. On the other hand, it is you, who can be a source of this information for others to change their behavior and to make them grow. You can have your own interest in it, as their behaviors can have a direct impact on you, so you want them to start or stop doing something. But you also want them just to grow because you care. You want them to be a better person just like that, without strings attached.

This book teaches you how to effectively communicate your needs and positively influence the behavior of those around you. Thanks to a few simple rules and learning techniques of effective feedback, you will be able to build better relationships with the people you care about and have your own needs satisfied as well. This applies to your relationships with your friends and family or your relationships at work. Regardless whether you will use the knowledge gained here in a conversation with a co-worker or your child or partner, you will notice a real improvement in the reception of your words. You'll gain a higher ratio of applying your advice.

Using the knowledge from this book, you will become aware how feedback can help you improve and how to use it to improve others. You'll even start to asking for one.

III. Forms of Feedback

Every action you carry out or statement you make has an effect on other people and on the environment. Any information about that effect, which comes back to you, is called a feedback. This is **information about the effect of your past action, which should influence your future action**. It is the environment's reaction to your action, which may come back to you in the form of oral or written statement from another person. It also could come in form of an action, body language, or through statistics. Below are some examples of situations where there was a feedback.

You told a joke in a group
and you saw how one person's face reddened.

This is an example of **non-verbal feedback**. By the reddened face, you realize the individual was not comfortable with the joke, although he did not say it explicitly. Facial expressions and non-verbal signals carry more meaning than words. Also, they are more natural and more difficult to hide.

You organized a training for volunteers
and there were a lot of people.

This an example of feedback that came back to you in the form of other people's **actions**. A large number of participants is likely an evidence that the time and subject are suitable for them, if not, they would not have come. Here, it is important to mention that this feedback may lead to further analysis. In many cases, you might have to quiz the participants. Maybe they came because there were free cookies and coffee.

*You were listening to loud music at home
and a neighbor asked you to turn it down.*

This is an example of the classic **verbal feedback**. This means someone told you directly how your behavior affected him. You will learn more about this kind of feedback later in this book. It has the advantage over others that it is often clear and understandable without additional questions. Unfortunately, this does not happen always.

You can use the knowledge from above in two separate ways. One is to start recognizing a feedback which comes to you from any side. Be aware of what people talk, but also how they talk, what is their mimic and what are their actions. All those channels can provide you with full of useful information about your behavior. So you can apply changes if you see them good. The second way is to use all those channels of feedback giving to provide your feedback to others. You can talk to them but also use your smile or attend their lecture if you think it is interesting. All kinds of small acts of giving a feedback will be appreciated sooner or later. The devil is in details.

Giving and receiving feedback is an art and working with the received feedback is the most important part of a personal development. The information people receive reminds them of the effect their actions has on those around them or on their environment at large. This way, they know whether what they had in mind when they did something is reflected in the results of actions.

If you are keen on your personal development, then learning how to work with feedback is an essential skill. It will eliminate the gap between your intentions and the actual effect of your actions. To put it straight — if you will work with feedback, you will act effectively and obtain the desired results.

The process of working with feedback goes like this:

Action ➔ *Effect* ➔ **Feedback** ➔ *Calibration*

Using this loop, you can modify your behavior until you get the result you desire. With this approach, it is only a matter of time that you begin to see the desired results. Every feedback and every adjustment according to the feedback will get you closer to success in your chosen field.

IV. Why You Should Give Feedback To Others

It is simple: **to make them grow**. But let put this into three categories as reasons depend on the situation.

Shape Human Behavior That Affects You

By giving someone a feedback, you shape his behavior which has a direct impact on you. When you give feedback on a positive behavior, you reinforce it and increase the chance of its repetition. If you are pleased with what someone has done, you want that person to keep doing that same thing. Appreciate that action by telling that person how it has affected you positively and how you feel about it. He will also feel nice and will most likely repeat this action in the future.

The same mechanism also operates in the case of negative behavior. When someone did something you didn't like, informing him helps to eliminate this behavior next time. Of course, your information may not always translate into an instant change. Everyone has the right not to change his habits and you have to respect that. However, particularly, in relationships with loved ones, you can be sure that they want the best for you. They would not purposely behave in a way to hurt you. If you, therefore, give a feedback, they will most likely want to improve the way they act.

Motivate and Inspire People to Action

By giving feedback, you can become a source of inspiration and motivation for people around you. Everyone wants to grow and be effective in what they do. Your feedback is a gift that you give to others. It's something they do not know about themselves and their behavior and it can really be useful to them. It's some kind of a mirror for what they do. Feedback can often be a powerful motivating tool. When it is well used, it can inspire others to action. For some people, correction motivates them to put in more work because they are ambitious. For others, correction can have a counterproductive effect, particularly in people with low self-esteem. In that case, it is better to appreciate something in which this person is better. Praise, however, motivates the vast majority of people. When praising an individual, it is important that it is about a particular situation and the contribution of the individual, not just about the result. Appreciating the efforts exerted is important especially in creative environments. It encourages more innovation and gives room for mistakes which would lead to better results. You should observe on your own which kind of feedback is most motivating in given situation.

Encourage Reciprocity

The principle of reciprocity will work. If you give someone a feedback, that person will be more willing to give it to you. Thus, you increase the chance of receiving feedback, which you need for your own development. Day after day you build an environment of openness. Paradoxically, by contributing to the development of others you also contribute to your own development. This is an excellent example of a win-win situation.

V. Four Rules of Effective Feedback

Facts and Opinions

At the beginning, you need to develop the habit of distinguishing opinions from facts and **speak only about facts**. Opinions are based on the subjective perception of reality and the feelings associated with an event or occurrence. Auditory, visual or sensory feelings received from the environment are filtered through the lens of your own life experiences. Whether something is „nice" or „ugly" depends entirely on your own beliefs and the thought patterns that you have acquired over time. Someone else may have an entirely different mindset, and will, therefore, perceive these things quite differently. That is the weakness of opinions — everyone has one's own. This is, however, different with facts. They are based on data that is perceived by various people in the same way. It is a fact that something lasted 10 minutes because this is the same value for everyone. The fact that for some, this is a very long time (for example, waiting in line at the store) and for others, it is short (for example, skiing), is purely their opinion. You can't argue with facts, it is absolute, while opinions are definitely debatable. If you want to avoid unnecessary discussions, and believe me, you want, always present facts.

Below are examples of situations where you can present facts.

Opinion: *You're always late.*

Fact: *You were late twice this week.*

Opinion: *This is ugly written.*

Fact: *I cannot read what is written here.*

Opinion: *You are doing a good job.*

Fact: *Thanks to your work, sales have jumped by 3%.*

Furthermore, talking about your feelings is factual as opposed to talking about the feelings of others. Your feelings are a fact. That you felt in one way or another, is not questionable. Nobody can say you did not feel it. Of course, this is your subjective feeling and not everyone in this situation would feel the same way. But the fact that you felt a certain way can make an impression on the person to whom you are giving feedback. If the individual cares about your feelings, he will take them into account, regardless of whether they are only your thoughts or they are repeated in the statements of others.

However, while talking about feelings of others, your response is filtered by your previous experience. You are passing each event through your own filter and interpreting it in your own way. For example, ask yourself how many times you carried out an activity with someone and after some time, when recalling the event, the two of you give different accounts. How is it possible that each of you experienced the same thing at the same time, and yet see the same event in two different ways?

First, this is because we all filter the events around us and our experience through the lens of our thought patterns and beliefs. If someone in your presence rests his feet on the desk, you can either see this as a sign of disrespect or that the person is simply trying to relax. The fact is that someone put his feet on the desk. How it will be received depends on the individual involved.

Furthermore, each of you focused on different things or sensations. Has it ever occurred to you, when you bought a particular brand of a car, that you will begin to notice that same brand more often? This is because you started to focus on that. It is sometimes unbelievable how the human brain operates selectively. Just do this simple exercise. Next time, when you are out on the road, pay attention to everything that is red. You will most certainly notice things that have been on the road for years that you never saw previously. The simple reason is that you are now focused on them.

Because each person has its own filters and focuses on different things you should always use facts as an argument instead of opinions.

The Perspective of „I" vs. The Perspective of „you"

Another important thing about giving feedback is to learn to distinguish between the perspective of *I* from the perspective of *you*. Everyone, in general, has a good opinion about himself and when making a decision believes that he is right. When you inform someone that he has done something wrong and he thinks otherwise, it causes an internal conflict. Such a person immediately start to defend himself and is not interested in listening anymore. You'll be amazed how often this mechanism is triggered, but it's a road to nowhere. The feedback, in this case, should be done from the perspective of *I*, which **generally talk about yourself** and your feelings. Telling someone how you feel after an event or speech will not cause the person to deny these feelings. No one can say you are not feeling what you are feeling. Therefore, to avoid confrontation in the case of a negative behavior, use the *I* perspective.

Example of *I* perspective [FACT]:
I felt unappreciated when you said that it was thanks to Mark.

We can see two things clearly here. First, the action took place in the past. Second, the effect this action had on the speaker. With the use of the *I* perspective, there is no room for confrontation.

In the case of a feedback on a positive behavior, make use of the *you* perspective. This way, you will show your sense of the value of the person. By appreciating the person involved and the efforts one have put in, you amplify the positive feedback. Since everyone has a good feeling about themselves, it will also increase the self-esteem of the persons concerned.

Example of *you* perspective [OPINION]:
I liked your speech. I see, that you did a lot of work.

With the use of the *you* perspective, you have been able to highlight what the person did right. But you don't really know how much work a person put in speech. You only suspect that.

Time

The elapsed time, between the event and the feedback about it, is important for the impact of that feedback. The general rule is **the sooner, the better**. This is due to the fact that immediately after the event, the feedback has the strongest influence. The human brain builds the strongest link between an event and its consequences when it knows these consequences immediately. Such connection of pain or pleasure is useful in your personal development. You associate behaviors that you want to stop with suffering, while you will associate behavior you want to encourage with pleasure. Some parents use this method to discourage their children from smoking. By telling a child to smoke the whole pack of cigarettes at once will often lead to that child vomiting and feeling unwell. This feeling occurs immediately and is so strong that such child associates cigarettes with suffering. Thus, most of them abstain from smoking. Rewards work in same way. It is not without reason that this method of rapid feedback is used to tame animals. After each command that is well done, the animal gets a treat. The treat is given only immediately after the job well done to bring about the desired effect. If the animal gets a delicacy a few minutes later, it will not completely connect the fact of getting the award with the task that was done. This mechanism works similarly for humans and animals. **Time plays a key role in giving feedback**. Don't wait until the person you are talking to, will forget the specific scenarios you are mentioning. Instead, for example, after leaving a meeting or after a conversation you should instantly share your feelings and the speaker will know exactly what situation you're talking about.

The exception to this rule is in the case of negative emotions. When they come into play in connection with an unpleasant situation, an emotional person is focused solely on the manifestation of their feelings and would not likely listen to what you are saying. If you have had to explain something to crying child, you will understand what I am writing about. I have had to do it from time to time. The child would not completely accept what he is told. Given that children more than adults show their emotions, it perfectly presents how this mechanism works. Adults also behave the same way, though usually, they do not manifest their emotions in such a visible way. In the situation like this, you should wait until negative emotions have abated. This could be an hour later or a day or several days later depending on the situation. You should certainly not delay feedback for weeks.

The response time for the behavior also affects the speed of learning. The faster feedback, the quicker someone will correct their behavior and learn how it impacts those around them. I remember my first time as a team coach. I often started working with my teams by pointing out the basic mistakes they make. I was convinced that they wanted to be a better team, so telling them about their mistakes at the beginning would be a great gift for them. Unfortunately, I was wrong. Nobody likes to be criticized, in particular by someone who just joined a team. It took me a quite a long time before I realized that you first have to establish a relationship with people and appreciate what they have already done well. Unfortunately, I never asked for a feedback early enough. This could have saved me many months of unnecessary clashes with teams. This is precisely the great power of early feedback.

Place

The place, where feedback is communicated, is crucial for its acceptance. Generally, the rule is: you give a **positive feedback in a group, while you give a negative feedback in private**.

First of all, the person concerned should feel comfortable in the place where you want to give a feedback. This applies to both positive and negative feedback. Often, praising someone in front of the entire team has the additional effect of strengthening the team. The person concerned knows that not only the person giving feedback knows about his positive behavior but others know. Sometimes, it encourages the person involved. It may, however, depressing for someone who is shy. Then it is better to do it alone. The attitude from group to this person is also important. If it is hostile, praising someone in front of others can make this hostility deeper. A little easier, however, is feedback on negative behavior. In this case, it is very rare to find reasons to do it in public. This should be done in private, face to face. You can select a small conference room or a private place if you want it to be very formal or meet for lunch. Often, informal meetings, such as lunch or just a night out for a beer can relieve tension and build a greater trust in the individual about your intention. Put yourself for a moment in his situation and think about where you would like to hear the words that you want to convey. Or, if it is possible, let the person concerned choose a place.

Exercises

Exercise 1. Facts and opinions

Which of the following statements are facts and which are opinions? Change every sentence you consider opinion into a sentence stating a fact. This will allow you to distinguish one from another.

- I do not like this idea.
- You did well on the presentation.
- You disregarded performing the task.
- You are too confident.
- You did a good job.
- I see that you are enthusiastic about this work.
- You did not plan the meeting I told you about.
- Your presentation made a big impression on me.
- I felt the positive energy at the meeting you set up.
- You're never on time.
- Everyone knows how to do it.
- You volunteered for this task.
- You have been on time for all meetings this week.

- You expressed your opinion about this project loudly.
- This week you were late three times.
- I felt ignored when you did not mention my name.
- Probably you spent a lot of time on this solution.
- You managed this task well.
- You're wrong.
- The floor in the kitchen is dirty.
- I feel bad when you talk to me in such a tone.
- I think you treated him well.
- You finished this task earlier than expected.
- You cleaned your room.
- You never look after yourself.
- You made me coffee.
- You offered me help.
- You helped me to move.
- You're always so prepared.
- You've spent dozen hours on this task.

Exercise 2. The perspective of „I" and the perspective of „you"

Which of the following statements are spoken from the perspective of *you*. Turn them into sentences spoken from the perspective of *I*. This exercise will help you to identify these perspectives and to use them in the appropriate situation.

- You're making a terrible mess.
- You are not dealing with it.
- It bothers me when you do it.
- You do not like me.
- I need your approval.
- You are always not present in such moments.
- You are rarely at home.
- I like it when you bring me flowers.
- It hurts me when you say so.

VI. The Techniques for Constructing Feedback

To construct a feedback you can use a predefined and proven technique or scheme. This will help you give feedback quickly and you will not forget important element. Below, I will show you three techniques that you can follow immediately. Remembering the elements involved in the technique while giving feedback will greatly increase your chances of success. As you begin to work with these techniques, they may seem unnatural at first. Don't worry about that. Keep practicing them until they become second nature. The elements of the techniques will come up in your discussions with the person you want to convey feedback. The order of the elements in given techniques does not really matter in practice and it varies according to the situation. Don't worry about it. It is important that you use each element, that's all. When giving feedback, the more elements of the techniques you introduce at the beginning of a conversation, the shorter it will be and the fewer questions will come up.

To learn these techniques, it is better to select one of the three methods described below and practice it until you are adept. Learning all three at once can be difficult and as a result, you may not remember any of them well.

Technique #1

FECE - Facts Emotions Consequences Expectations

Yesterday, you came out of a status meeting before the end. I was counting on your support to the end. After you left, I was uncomfortable. It was impossible for me to focus on the presentation and I did not say what I prepared. I propose that next time we will agree before the meeting when one of us can go out. Is it OK?

Facts: You start from the description of a particular event or situation that you do not like. Remember to use the facts, what happened and when it happened.

Yesterday, you came out of a status meeting before the end

Emotions: Then review how you felt in connection with this event or situation.

I was hoping for your support to the end and then I felt uncomfortable

Consequences: Mention what the action affected and what happened because of the way you were feeling. Sometimes the consequences coincide with the feelings. If this happens, you can skip this step.

It was impossible for me to focus on the presentation and I did not say what I prepared.

Expectations: Mention exactly what you need to feel comfortable in such situations.

I propose that next time we will agree before the meeting when one of us can go out.

This method contains all necessary elements to construct a proper feedback. The order of these elements is not important. In practice, you will notice that it will change depending on the situation. If you omit any of the components, especially when giving a feedback on a negative behavior, you can be sure that sooner or later it will appear in the conversation. People will inquire what you expect them to do in that situation, or what this behavior really affected. Thinking about this before and saying it as a whole, leads to a shorter discussion about the topic. And this is the whole point of the technique, to convey feedback briefly and directly.

Technique #2

SBI - Situation, Behavior, Impact

Last night, as we were having dinner at a pizzeria, you offered to help me in the execution of my idea. I felt supported and this gave me the motivation to keep working. Thanks.

Situation: Mention the specific situation, time and place so the person concerned knows exactly what you mean. So it's best to do it immediately after the incident.

Last night, as we were having dinner in a pizzeria

Behavior: Describe the behavior that affected you.

You offered to help me in the execution of my idea

Impact: Mention how the action affected you. Talk about your feelings. It's a fact that you felt something. No one can accuse you that you did not feel that way.

I felt supported and this gave me the motivation to continue working. Thanks

This method, due to the lack of expectations, can be applied in situations where the chances of meeting the person again are small. This may be a situation in a shop or on the bus. You want someone to pay attention to something, but the expectation of something in the future is inconsequential because you will probably never meet again. This method can also be used for obvious events. The fact that you notice a behavior and mention the consequences are enough for the person concerned to know what to do next. In this case, there is no need to inform a person what is expected of him or how bad what he did was.

Technique #3

COIN: Connect It, Observations, Impact and Next Steps

I know that your goal for this month is to deliver working software to your clients. You mentioned recently that you have a slight delay. I also noticed that you decided to change technology, which makes me a little worried. According to estimates, those changes will extend the project by nearly 20%. I wish that in the future we will make such decisions together to work out the best solution.

Connect it: Establish the goals and interests. Build context.

I know that your goal for this month is to deliver working software to client

Observations: Describe your specific insights about the behavior. Deal with facts.

I also noticed that you decided to change technology, which makes me a little worried

Impact: Describe the impact that this behavior had on you or on the work and goals of the individual.

According to estimates, it will extend the project by nearly 20%.

Next Steps: Suggest a proposal for improvements. Set a goal to which the person can aspire, leaving how to achieve the goal to the individual unless he asks for your help.

I wish that in the future we will make such decisions together to work out the optimum solution.

This method can be successfully applied in the business environment, for example, during a performance appraisal. It contains elements of both the observed behavior as well as a proposal for improvements. Remember, when proposing solutions, to focus on the goals that the person has to achieve. Give room for creativity by letting the person decide how to achieve the goal. By this, you will boost the person's motivation. You will definitely be surprised by the creative solutions that will come up.

Exercise. Remember the methods of constructing a feedback

I know from experience that people who hear about these methods in our training soon forget what these abbreviations mean. My desire is that after reading this book, you will remember at least one of the three methods described above. I will focus on technique #1. That is why I am showing you in a few steps how to remember it using memory techniques. This simple exercise will make you remember this technique for a long time.

1. Select one of the three methods described above. The one that seems easiest to you that you could easily apply at work or at home.

2. In your mind, associate abstract words such as 'fact' that are difficult to visualize, feel or touch, with something physical and perceptible by the senses. For example, for me, the word 'facts' is associated with a newspaper, the word 'feelings' with crying woman, 'consequences' with spilled milk and 'expectations' with the printed range of my duties.

3. Task your imagination and make up a story using the associations you came up with. Mine is as follows.

   The newspaper is on the table, crying woman walks up to it and begins to wipe her eyes with a newspaper. The newspaper becomes very wet that it can be twisted. Her tears are flowing like a river. The crying woman pours milk on her head. The milk is in a bottle made of A4 paper on which is printed the range of my duties.

4. Remind yourself of this story over the next few days. This will help you to easily remember the technique when you want to give a feedback.

VII. Providing Feedback on Positive Behaviors

How to recognize areas, which are praise-worthy.

One thing I have observed is the fact that some people do not know how to acknowledge the positive things in others. A lot of times I hear statements like, „How do I find something positive in him since everything he does makes me nervous?". Or directly with a seemingly honest statement, „She has nothing positive in her". Remember this rule once and for all: if you cannot see it, that doesn't mean it does not exist. You have probably never seen the Fiji Islands before but you know it is located somewhere in the world. The people with whom fate tied you in some way, which you have not related positively with certainly have a whole range of positive qualities. Note that these people often have a partner, children or friends. They would not have these relationships if they were bad to the bone. So, avoid questions such as, „Has he got any positive qualities?". Instead, ask yourself, „What are the positive traits he has, which I cannot see now?". Pay more attention to the strengths of the person and how to improve your own observation of the positive qualities in people.

Appreciating the other person is the basis for building a relationship, which in turn directly impacts on the effectiveness of the feedback you give him. When you compliment someone about his behavior, you help him and you help yourself as well. He feels good about himself and that increase the chances of him repeating such behavior in the future.

Appreciating people may not come easy for you but you would have to develop the habit. If you want people to appreciate you, then you have to do it first. Therefore, at the end of this chapter, I suggest a set of two tools and one challenge that will help you learn to appreciate others better. Being able to appreciate others is a critical step if you want to influence others positively.

Motivation by Appreciation

By letting people know that their actions have a positive impact, you motivate them to do more of it. Perhaps you may not have realized it but sometimes your encouragement may determine whether or not people continue in a course of action or not. There have probably been times when you were thinking of doing something, and you asked a loved one for advice. And you knew their opinion will determine whether or not you will follow through with that idea or abandon it. You also have the same influence on others. If someone did something for the first time and is not sure he wants to go in this direction, your compliments can be a deciding factor if he would continue or abandon that path. You have the ability to have a positive influence on people, why not use it?

Let me add, that **what should be appreciated is the effort that has been put in and not only the results**. It's very easy to be demotivated after putting lots of efforts with little results to show for it. In that case, you need to acknowledge the efforts that have been put in so far. This will encourage the individual to try even harder next time. Making mistakes is an integral part of learning. The more mistakes made in the process of learning, the better you get at a particular skill. An easy example would be in teaching children. It is not particularly important whether the sun and the clouds, which a child painted, actually resembles the real thing. The more important thing is the efforts the child puts in. If you evaluate the result alone, you tell the child that trying is not worth it, because nothing came out of it. However, acknowledging the efforts he has put in, you let the child know that the time spent painting was not a waste. By spending time on the skill, the child would sooner or later get significantly better results. This applies to employees in organizations as well. Appreciating the efforts put in and not just the end results always lead to increased productivity.

I do not mean that results or the achievement of goals are not important. Of course, they are, and you should take them into consideration. My point, however, is that it is effort and lessons learned from failures that lead to better results. Focusing solely on the results does not tell the employee anything about how to get these results. Appreciating their efforts, however, gives a clear signal that what they are doing will eventually lead to the achievement of their goals.

This principle also applies to giving compliments. For example, you saw an attractive lady and you told her that she is dressed very nicely. She will probably appreciate the compliment. But what you have really done is to compliment the dress (and indirectly designer) and not the woman. So how do you compliment her in a way that would really acknowledge her? To do that, you apply the rule described above: appreciate the individual's efforts. You could consider any of the following.

You matched great shoes to your dress.

I see that you spent long hours on your fingernails — the effect is phenomenal.

In each case, you have acknowledged the efforts that she has put into her appearance and therefore, able to connect with her at a deeper level.

Traps to avoid when giving praise

Trap #1: The perspective of „I"

Here, in contrast to giving feedback on a negative behavior, you want to emphasize the other person's perspective. You can talk about your feelings and about the impression something made on you. At the same time, however, you want to appreciate the person's efforts. For example, although sometimes you are full of good intentions, when you make statements like, „I am proud of you", you have not directly acknowledged the person involved. You can, however, be direct with your compliment when you acknowledge the efforts that have been put in.

Consider the following sentences.

You helped me in carrying luggage.

You did a good job which will help our accounting of funds.

You inspired me to take on public speaking.

Trap #2: Dishonesty

It is important to be sincere when giving feedback. Insincerity can be quickly detected and your compliments will be counterproductive. This can lead to a breakdown of trust. And it is difficult to win someone's confidence after trust is breached. The truth is no one likes to be manipulated. There are better ways to ensure that someone is sincerely appreciated. You just need to take the time to look for things that you can truly compliment. This effort will definitely pay off. You might have been in a situation when someone begins to shower you with compliments. Only for the real intentions of this unusual behavior to be clear when the person comes asking for a favor. You should beware of such situations and try not to do so yourself. Manipulation and insincerity kill relationships!

Trap #3: Procrastination

With each passing day after the event, the impact of your feedback decreases, so it is important to pass it without delay. Compliments which were given, say a month after the event, will have little or no value and may sound strange or artificial. Your feedback will have a maximum impact if you give it immediately. Imagine that you presented a speech that pushed you beyond the comfort zone and took a lot of preparation. Someone then walks up to you a month later telling you that he liked the speech. If you had not received a positive feedback earlier on, you are likely to have a negative opinion about your performance. Such feedback given after a month might do little to change the negative opinion you might have had about the performance. The point is that people make their conclusions about an event immediately after it. You can use this to help others by giving positive feedback immediately after an event. Do not count on someone else to do it. Most often, others are hoping that someone else will do and then nobody says anything. Do not allow such situation by delaying feedback. Give it right away.

Exercises

Exercise 1. Change your thinking

The next time you meet someone you find difficult to see any positive quality in, think about the person in a different context than the one in which your current relationship operates. For example, if he is your boss or someone from work, think of him as a father or perhaps as a son to his parents. Try to visualize him in settings other than the work environment. Such a simple visualization will help you see the person differently and open a way to see his positive qualities.

Exercise 2. Start with yourself

Before you look for positive qualities in other people, turn the searchlight on yourself. This exercise will make you discover areas of life which you will pay attention to later in others. For example, your strength may be good manners, you can look out for this in someone else. Perhaps the person is lazy but has good manners that you can appreciate. This exercise will also show you how many positive attributes you have yourself and will definitely raise your self-esteem.

Take a pen and paper and write down the most important roles that you play at this moment in your life. For me, it would be husband, father, entrepreneur, runner, friend and author. Write down yours and under each of them, write down your positive traits in each of these contexts and what you have achieved. Then read everything again. This will help you see so many good things about you.

The Challenge: For next 10 days, look out for positive attributes in others.

1. Set a goal that every day you will give someone feedback on something they have done right or simply appreciate someone. No matter how small, but be honest. Start with a goal as small as one praise a day.

2. During the day, look for little things that your co-workers, friends, family or strangers do that affected you positively. Then, appreciate them verbally, by email or by telephone.

3. Continue this exercise for 10 consecutive days.

    After 10 days, you will realize that appreciating the little things that others do become easier for you. You will also see how this little praise each day affects you and the people that you praised. Initially, some of them may be surprised by your words. Especially if you previously have had problems with praising others. You may hear questions like, „Ok, what do you need from me?". Let them know that your intentions are sincere and that you are simply working on your self-development.

VIII. Providing Feedback on Negative Behaviors

How to talk about the negative behaviors

Many people have difficulties letting others know when they have done something wrong. There are some reasons for this. The most common reason is that they are afraid that speaking up might affect their relationship negatively. They are not sure how the other party will respond or they are even confident that it will be a stormy session. In this chapter, I will give you some practical tips on how to make this process easier for you and for the person you are talking to. Of course, a lot depends on the character and temperaments of the persons involved, but these few tips can minimize the risk that someone will feel offended by what you say and thus increase your effectiveness.

- Be direct about your feelings and about the impact of the person's behavior on you. Avoid the use of the word *you*. Talk about yourself, your feelings and needs.
  Wrong: *You could sometimes clean up your desk!*
  Right: *I feel uncomfortable when there is a mess here. I would feel much better if you will clean up the desk from time to time. Can we arrange that?*

- Talk about the behavior of the person, not about him. The person is not unreasonable, but only acted unwisely. This is a huge difference between the two. We all make mistakes every now and then. Even if such behavior is repeated, saying the person is unreasonable only makes him do that again. Telling someone constantly how bad he is in doing something, makes him believe it and use it as an excuse for his further mistakes.

  Wrong: *You are inaccurate.*

  Right: *You missed some details on this project.*

- Avoid generalizations. Feedback should only relate to one event, not the fact that someone is always doing something. For example, instead of saying „you are always late", simply make reference to the specific examples of lateness and let the person know what will happen as a result. I remember one event in a team I coached. Every day we met at 9 am to plan the day. I noticed that one particular member of the team was coming late for the meeting. After some time, I went up to him and told him my observations that he is always late, suggesting that we can shift the hour of the meeting to better suit him. He, however, disagreed saying he had not been late. I didn't know what to say. In response to that, I hung a weekly chart on the wall and, for the whole next week, I inscribed an „X" each time he was late. I did it openly, so he was also able to see it. After a week, I went up to him and told him he had been late three times in the past week and therefore we were postponing the time of the meeting. He admitted that I was right and that he actually had a problem with the time of the meeting. Always use data if you can get one.

Wrong: *You are always late.*

Right: *You were late this morning so the meeting was delayed and the rest of us had to wait for you.*

- Address the issue when both of you are relaxed but do not let be too far away from when the event occurred. Do not delay more than is necessary. Tell the person right away when something is bothering you. Sometimes, the person involved is aware of the situation and is waiting for your reaction. Each passing day that you delay your feedback only builds up unnecessary tension in him. Moreover, such person may already prepare how to defend himself. The quicker you relay your feedback, the more complications you avoid and the more effective your feedback is.

- Find a place where both of you feel comfortable and can talk to each other. If it is possible, let it be a neutral place, such as lunch outside the company or an evening meeting over drinks.

- Avoid mixing messages and „sandwich" techniques (first positive, then negative, and at the end again positive). It is very confusing to the person you are giving a feedback. If you have a feedback about a negative behavior, just pass it. Do not try to „lessen the effect" by adding artificial praises. There have been cases where a boss so softly tried to approach the message of firing someone that the person didn't even know he has been fired. Give only one information at a time. That way, you will avoid misunderstandings.

The difference between criticism and feedback

It is important to know the difference between criticizing someone and giving a constructive feedback. Only the latter will help you have a real impact on the people around you and make them listen to you. Here are a few elements of criticism.

- Generalizations

   In particular with respect to time (always, never, sometimes), places (everywhere, nowhere) and persons (everyone, no one) are the words characteristic of criticism. Consider the following sentences.

   You're always late.

   You never take care of yourself.

   You are never here when I need you.

   Everyone knows how to do it.

   These are all examples of criticisms. That is because they lack specificity. Meanwhile, a constructive feedback refers to the specific situation.

- The brevity of expression

  All you hear in criticism is an expression of what a person has done wrong and no information on the effect of his behavior or what the right behavior should be. Sentences from the above point are perfect examples. Remember that by criticizing someone you are not teaching him what is right. You are only indicating what he has done wrong. These two are not the same. Mentioning only what someone has done wrong and not correcting them is not actually useful.

- A reference to a person and not an event

  Critics often talk about the person and not about his behavior. Consider the following statements.

  Do you have to be so laggard?

  You're foolish for doing that.

  You were again inaccurate in calculations.

  These statements all point to the personality involved. They are dangerous for two reasons. First, they evoke immediate defensive reactions, which causes your statement to lose its effectiveness. What's more is that they often lead to unnecessary quarrels. Secondly, it addresses the personality which controls the behavior. And it is very hard to change someone's personality.

  A reference to a person's personality will not bring you the expected results but may backfire. When you frequently tell someone that he is „laggard", he begins to believe it, and see himself as that. When this occurs, each subsequent delay he will be explained with the fact that „he is simply a laggard and will therefore always be late". He will begin to believe that he is laggard and that nothing can change it.

Examples of criticism.
You always spoil everything.
I can never rely on you.
You did not do it well.
You are irresponsible.

A well-formulated feedback, on the other hand, is the opposite of criticism and is characterized by the following elements.

- A specific time and place of the event.
  Instead of generalizations, use the location of an event or series of events in time and space.

- Expanded statement
  Constructive feedback provides information on the impact of behavior on others, and it often requires a few sentences. Furthermore, it includes expectations to the person and suggestions for improvement.

- Appeal to a specific behavior

  Constructive feedback refers to a specific behavior or series of behaviors, but never to the person personally. Often data in form of figures is collected earlier to visualize to the person involved the extent of his behavior and the consequences. Constructive feedback is based wholly on facts.

- Use the *I* perspective instead of the *you* perspective.

  You specify what happened and how it affected you. Talk about your feelings, not only about the behavior of the other party.

Examples of a constructive feedback.

Yesterday I attended your seminar on communication. I really liked it and learned several techniques that can be useful to me. Thanks. You should organize more of such seminars.

We sit close together and I can hear what you are playing in your headphone. Because of that, I can't concentrate on my work. Could you please turn it down?

Several times this week, when I returned home with the son from kindergarten, I find it hard to open the passenger door of the car, because your car is parked very close to mine. Would it be a problem for you to leave a little more space between our cars?

Exercises

Exercise 1. A person or event

Change the following sentences to speak about a specific incident and not about a person or his character. You will practice separating the assessment of a person's behavior from the person.

- *You are unreasonable.*
- *You are laggard.*
- *You are irresponsible.*
- *You are scatterbrained.*

Exercise 2. Generalizations

Modify the following sentences so that it talks about facts and the specific situation. Generalizations are the bane of incorrect feedback. This exercise will help you distinguish generalizations from specific situations.

- *You are always late.*
- *You never look after yourself.*
- *You always react that way.*
- *You always throw your clothes everywhere.*

IX. Receiving Feedback

Accepting feedback, though often underestimated, is also an art, and has a substantial impact on your relationships with others. You need to realize that giving feedback is not always easy especially when it is about negative behavior. How you react to this information may determine the trajectory of your relationship. That is why it is important to receive feedback correctly, both on good behavior, and on bad behavior. Special attention is however required in the case of the latter. When you are able to receive feedback well, it builds confidence in the other party and makes him more willing to give you feedback. One thing that will make it easier for you to accept feedback, even on negative behavior, is to realize that feedback is a gift. After all, if not for this information, you will never know what impact your behavior is having on those around you. When you begin to see it this way, your attitude to such information will change dramatically. Not only you will be grateful but you will be curious about what people have to say about you.

Below is a scheme that illustrates how to correctly receive feedback, once somebody provided you one:

Appreciate the feedback ➔ *Clarify the feedback* ➔ *Check with your intention* ➔ *Create an action plan*

Step #1: Appreciation

This is the first step in receiving feedback and it is the most important. It can be compared to the first impression when you meet someone. Remember that first impressions last long. How you start a conversation after receiving feedback will seriously affect how others would receive you. This is a decisive moment in which you show your commitment to your self-development. It would also show if you care about how you are perceived by others. Furthermore, your first reaction also shows your emotional maturity. You may react in an instinctive way, where your emotions take charge, or in a more thoughtful manner.

Perhaps it may seem trivial, but the easiest way to respond is with the words „thank you" or with the more elaborate version „thank you for telling me this". I know this can be difficult especially with a feedback on the negative behavior. Therefore, the appreciation does not always take the form of words, „thank you". It's about appreciating the fact that someone came and told you about the impact of your behavior on others giving you room for more growth. How you receive the feedback will determine if the person would want to give you feedback later in the future or if the person would be offended and not come back.

You can consider any of the following sentences to appreciate a feedback.

- *It's nice that you are telling me this.*
- *Thank you for telling me.*
- *I appreciate you called my attention to it.*
- *I did not realize it, that's good you told me this.*

Remember that every human action is directed toward a particular end, that is, the value the action is expected to bring. People stop doing a thing if it stops to bring them value. This is how we develop habits. Each one is built from exactly the same three parts: guideline, action, and reward. A guideline is anything that triggers the habit. This may be a driveway in a subway station, a determined hour, the alarm bell or seeing a loved one. An action is an activity carried out. The reward is the prize that is gotten for carrying out an action. In the context of this discussion, we would consider the prize. If somebody comes to you with a feedback and this act is appreciated by you verbally or through a change in behavior, this will be a kind of reward for feedback giver. Thus, this person will begin to develop the habit of giving you feedback. By appreciating the person, you will cause him to connect giving you feedback with something pleasant. This will encourage him to do that more often. Unfortunately, the converse of this is also true. If someone has the courage to give you feedback about a negative behavior, and he is punished for it in the form of your nervousness or a few bitter words, he will begin to associate giving you feedback with something unpleasant. In this case, he will not continue and you will have inadvertently closed one of the paths to your growth. Be aware of this.

Step #2: Clarification

Let's be straight. In the vast majority of cases you will experience, the feedback you will receive, will be way different from those described in this book. Most people will not stick to rules of giving feedback. They will skip the important elements such as stating their expectations. Some will direct their words at your personality and not about your behavior. All this does not change the fact that someone wants to communicate a feedback to you. And how well you will act in response to the feedback depends largely on you clarifying the comments. When a feedback is not precise, it's not particularly useful.

When it comes to feedback, different people do it differently. In some cases, there are extroverts who will flood you with information about their feelings and you will have to pick out the most useful information. In other cases, you may encounter introverts who, despite their deep thoughts, will only express themselves in a few words. Then you will have to dig deep so as to know what is in their mind. It is, therefore, important that when you receive feedback that you ask questions to understand exactly what the other person is saying, and what his expectations are.

To get the most important facts, you can ask these questions.

- *What did I do that you liked / did not like?*
- *Can tell me in one sentence the effect of my behavior?*
- *How do you feel about what I did?*

In a situation in which you need to get information, use the following questions.

- *I know you want to tell me something important, what is it?*
- *What's really bothering you?*
- *What in particular made the biggest impression on you?*

Example

Person A: I'm not sure of the way you are testing this product.

Person B: What exactly do you mean?

Person A: The clicking takes a long time. Can it be faster?

Person B: So you are suggesting to shorten the time?

Person A: That would be a good start.

Person B: What else caught your attention in the testing process?

Person A: Well, nothing, what I have said is the most important thing.

Person B: It's nice that you said that. I'll see what I can do.

The statement, *I'm not sure of the way you are testing this product*, does not really say much. However, after clarifying the feedback, more useful information is gotten.

Step #3: Checking with your Intention

Feedback reveals how those in your environments perceives your actions. But only you knows the intentions behind your actions. Your role is to assess your intentions in the light of the feedback you received and see if they are consistent. If they are, it means that your actions are right and what you are doing is working. If the feedback you get do not match what you set out to achieve in the first place, that gives you an opportunity to correct yourself.

In the case where the final outcome was not what you intended, and someone around you was negatively impacted or hurt, you should just mention it. It shouldn't be a long story. Explain briefly that hurting the person was not your intention, perhaps you expressed yourself wrong. Let the person know what you wanted to achieve, apologize and move on.

Let me illustrate with an example. Say, you conducted a training seminar and your intention was to teach the participants a particular concept.

If for example, after the seminar, the participants mentioned that they did not learn anything new, this means you did not achieve your goal. Your methods have proven to be ineffective, so next time, you need to modify them to achieve success.

If on the other hand, you get feedback from the participants that they learned a lot from the seminar, it's a clear indication to you that your chosen methods work, and are in line with specified intentions. So, you can then repeat them next time.

Step #4: The Plan for further action

When you plan for further action, you must take note of two things: a plan of action and inform the person who gave you the feedback about the action plan. The first one is important for you and for your personal development. The second is important for the person who gave you the feedback and the relationship you have with each other. If someone gives you a feedback, he would usually expect you do something with the information. Informing such a person about your action plan would motivate him to give you more feedback.

Develop an action plan when your intentions fail to match with the feedback you receive about your actions. The more the intentions and the feedback are consistent, the more impact you make on those around you. This is the essence of feedback. It allows you to gain knowledge that can help you act effectively.

An important fact to remember is that you need to be yourself. You cannot live someone else's life. You can't always please those around you. If someone expects you to do things that you think are beyond the scope of your duties, tell him directly.

Consider the following scenario:

Employee: Hi. I feel that you do not always solve the problems that I bring to you. I want you to deal with these issues because they are important to me.

Manager: Thanks for the information, and I appreciate that you spoke you mind. I am however seeing it in a different light. My role as your manager is to support you in solving problems, not to solve them for you. I would like you to deal with the important things yourself and be responsible for them. From my part, I will support you if the situation will require the use of management tools, or if you just want to talk about options and solutions.

Employee: I understand. In that case, I would be happy to meet with you, the next time I get stuck.

Manager: Yeah, anytime.

But on the other hand, if you agree with the feedback and really want to change your behavior, you can start with these questions to your interlocutor:

- *So how would you solve this problem?*
- *How else can I behave next time?*
- *How can I still improve it?*

Remember to evaluate your actions once you apply correction on them. Ask if what you have done have improved that situation. This is important.

Improvement is a continuous process. You will constantly change something, and still, you will receive feedback on these behaviors. The cycle of action, feedback and correction based on feedback lead to continuous improvement.

X. Summary

This book was written based on my own professional experience as a team coach and player in the corporate world, as well as being a husband, father, friend, and the average Joe next door. In each of these roles I use the basic principles described above. These are the absolute basics of healthy communication with people, regardless of their age, sex or social position.

Giving feedback effectively requires some tact and skill. It's more of an art than science. There is no single recipe that works for all cases. Each of them will be different because every person and every relationship are different. The real skill is, therefore, adapting the knowledge you have acquired to the situation. Learn good communication patterns from this book but also use your intuition.

Think of this book as a reference guide that you will look up from time to time. Practice what you have learned in this book regularly to have a positive impact on your life and life of others. **Make them grow**. Share this book with friends. The more people who give positive feedback around you the better lives you all will have.

I want this book to be a better help for all those, who want to communicate with proper feedback. That's why I ask you kindly to write me feedback on this book, and how reading it has helped your communications and relationships. I want to know if my intentions met reality. For you, it will be some kind of real life test of what you've learned by reading. Thank you.

www.ingramcontent.com/pod-product-compliance
Lightning Source LLC
Chambersburg PA
CBHW061215180526
45170CB00003B/1013